Arieh
THE LION OF MEGIDDO

J. Spencer Bloch

Illustrations by Rony Tamir

Hello, everyone, my name is Arieh!
I'm the Lion of Megiddo, your guide today.
Come and learn about my town—it's high up on a hill,
Where the sounds of battles long ago echo still.

The Jezreel Valley is below us, so green and lush,
And the Way of the Sea, where the traders would rush.
The Canaanite princes here put me on their throne.
Eagle's wing, a human face—all made of stone.

To fight, they sharpened their sword and their arrow,
But found they couldn't beat Thutmose the Pharaoh.
Until "like a great lion" from Egypt went free,
The Israelite nation, all the way to Galilee.

I watched over them from here, from my lofty den,
Until the lion cub of Judah was born in Bethlehem.
David was his name, and Solomon his heir,
A lion stood on each side of his gold-and-ivory chair.

Megiddo was magnificent during the reign of the Jewish kings
A jasper image of me roaring was on their servants' rings!
With gate and fort and palace court, and cistern and stable;
I made friends with all the horses, whenever I was able.

Napoleon told me, when he saw Megiddo's worth.
"It is the most natural battleground upon the whole earth."
Then Field Marshal Allenby won it, during the Great War.
And on the Arms of England? Three lions like me roar!

I fought for Israel's freedom, and it became a state.
As the prophets promised – but just you wait!
The greatest battle is yet to be; then the ground will redden
Mt. Megiddo is better known by the name of Armageddon.

In the final battle of Gog and Magog, the Messiah will arrive,
To vanquish every evildoer and make our hopes survive.
Are you looking forward to it? I surely know I am.
For then, we lions will lie together with the lamb.

Copyright 2015
J. Spencer Bloch

All rights reserved. No part of the book may be used or reproduced by any means, graphic, electronic, or mechanical, including photocopying, recording, taping or by any information storage retrieval system without the written permission of the publisher, except in the case of brief quotations embodied in critical articles and reviews.

ISBN: 978-965-7607-30-5

Printed by  GESTELIT
info@gestelit.co.il
Printed in the Holy Land

Also in this series:

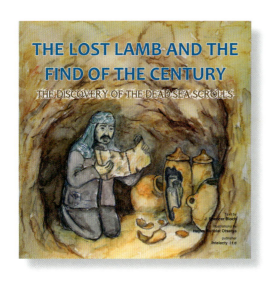
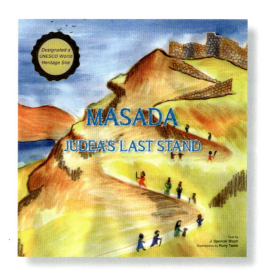

For ordering information, please contact the publisher:
Intelecty, Ltd.
76 Hagalil
Nofit, Israel 36001
Tel: 97249930922
Fax: 972722830147
Mobile: 972523348598
galit@gestelit.co.il
www.jesusbooks4kids.com